The Adventure C
OF THE WORLD

Rob Waring, *Series Editor*

HEINLE
CENGAGE Learning™

Australia • Brazil • Japan • Korea • Mexico • Singapore • Spain • United Kingdom • United States

Words to Know

This story is set in New Zealand. It happens far from the real capital of Wellington in a place known as the capital, or center, of adventure— Queenstown [kwinztaʊn].

 Adventure in the Air. Read the paragraph and look at the picture. Then match each word or phrase with the correct definition.

In Queenstown, New Zealand, adventure sports are usually fast, fun, and sometimes dangerous. Some local people do them as pastimes to have fun in their free time. Visitors often go to Queenstown to do them. Some people go bungee [bʌndʒi] jumping from the bridges over rivers. Other people hike into the mountains, and then ride back in a helicopter.

1. adventure _____	**a.** a kind of aircraft that has large turning blades
2. pastime _____	**b.** a structure used to cross over something
3. bungee jumping _____	**c.** an exciting and dangerous experience
4. bridge _____	**d.** take a long walk in a natural area
5. hike _____	**e.** an activity done when not working
6. helicopter _____	**f.** a sport in which people jump from a high place with a special rope

river

B **Adventure on the Water.** Read the sentences and then complete the paragraph with the underlined words.

Frightening means something makes you afraid.
A jetboat is a kind of boat that goes extremely fast.
A propeller turns around in the water to move a boat.
Shallow describes water which is not deep.
A thrill is a strong feeling of excitement and pleasure.

One popular pastime in Queenstown is riding in a (1)_____. Some people get a (2)_____ from the speed when they go very fast. This type of boat does not move with a (3)_____, so people can drive it in very little, or (4)_____, water. Driving a jetboat, like bungee jumping, can be a little (5)_____, but some people really like that!

A Jetboat

bungee jumping

helicopter

special rope

New Zealand is a land of many beautiful and quiet natural places, but Queenstown isn't one of them. "Ahh!" shouts one young man as he speeds toward the earth. Don't worry, he's not **crazy**,[1] he's bungee jumping! You can hear the cries of several more people as they jump from the Nevis High Wire Bungee site.

People come from around the world to do adventure sports in Queenstown—especially bungee jumping. Henry Van Asch is a worker at the jump site. He offers one reason why this site is so popular. "The **gap**[2] from the underside of that little silver **jump pod**[3] out there," he says as he points to the jump spot, "is 134 meters, which is about 440 feet." That's a long way down! The sport must be really fun because there are many people waiting for a chance to do it. What do they feel like before a jump?

---

[1] **crazy:** not having a good mind; not normal
[2] **gap:** distance between two objects
[3] **jump pod:** small container supported by metal wire from which people bungee jump

 CD 1, Track 07

metal wires

NEVIS HIGH WIRE BUNGEE
134m

jump pod

The Nevis High Wire Bungee Site

Most people can hardly wait to go. "I'm so ready! **Bring it on**!"[4] says one young man as he and his friends wait for their turn. Bungee jumping isn't just for men either; women also enjoy this adventure sport. "I'm getting excited, actually," says a young woman who is waiting for her jump time.

As the instructor gets the next person ready, he counts down to the jump: "Five, four, three, two, one!" The man jumps out of the pod and starts the 134-meter drop to the river. It looks like he's going to hit the ground! Then, suddenly he's pulled back up by the special rope, or bungee cord, that's connected to his legs. Whew!

If you like exciting adventure sports, New Zealand is the place to do them. Henry Van Asch explains why he thinks they are so popular. He says that the way of life, or lifestyle, of the people here is very adventurous. "New Zealand people have a very **immediate lifestyle**[5] a lot of the time," he says, "and that's what people can experience when they come here."

---

[4]**bring it on:** *(slang)* 'let's start'
[5]**immediate lifestyle:** *(uncommon use)* here the speaker may mean a risky or adventurous way of living

There's more than just bungee jumping to do in New Zealand. Visitors can also go for a jetboat ride. Riding in a jetboat is a special experience. As one jetboat driver says, "Ha! [There's] nothing like it!" The jetboat is another one of New Zealand's adventure **inventions**.[6] There's no propeller, so the boats can work in shallow water. They can also turn around in a very small space. "These machines…you can **spin 'em on a dime**!"[7] the jetboat driver says as he turns the boat around quickly.

Jetboats were especially designed to get around New Zealand's shallow rivers, but they're also really good at giving customers a thrill. "Ha ha ha! Yee hee hee!" cries the driver, as he enjoys the speed of the boat. "This is one of the number-one pastimes of people coming to New Zealand … more importantly probably [of people coming to] Queenstown," he explains when he finally stops for a rest.

---

[6]**invention:** something new that has never been made before
[7]**spin 'em on a dime:** *(slang)* turn the boats around in a small amount of space

Jetboat rides are a thrilling adventure sport in New Zealand.

In New Zealand, it seems that nearly every day someone creates another adventure sport. David Kennedy , who is from a company called 'Destination Queenstown', talks about just how many adventure sports there are to do: "You know, we quite **proudly**[8] call ourselves 'The Adventure Capital of the World,'" he says. He then adds, "There are so many adventure activities to do here. In fact, we worked it out that if you did one of every type of activity, you'd be here for sixty days!"

---

[8]**proud:** pleased or satisfied with a person, object or action

One of the newest adventures in Queenstown involves a five-hour hike up a mountain. It's hard work, but fun for everyone. The best part is, at the end of the hike, the hikers don't have to walk all the way down again. How do they get back? A guide for this adventure explains. "We'll stay here for ten minutes or so … fifteen minutes," he says, "Then we'll jump in the helicopter and fly back to Queenstown." The helicopter turns the five-hour hike into a five-minute flight back to the city!

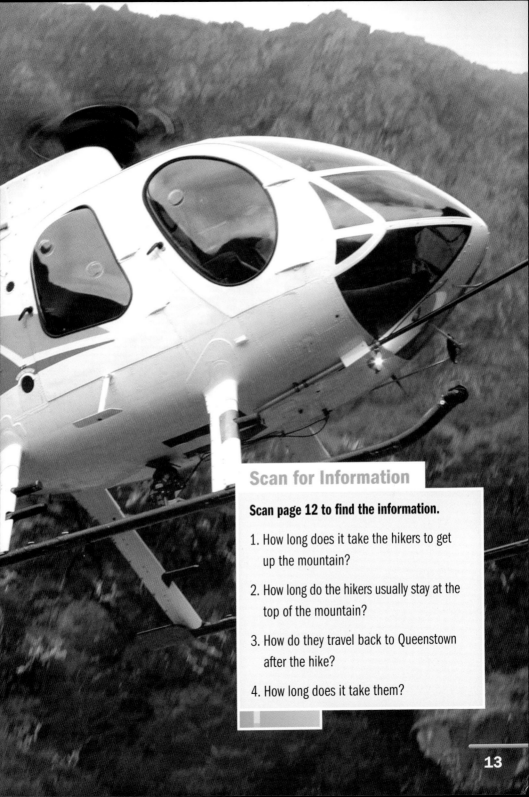

Scan for Information

Scan page 12 to find the information.

1. How long does it take the hikers to get up the mountain?

2. How long do the hikers usually stay at the top of the mountain?

3. How do they travel back to Queenstown after the hike?

4. How long does it take them?

The Kawarau Bridge

All of these different adventure sports really help the tourism industry in New Zealand. They're also part of an adventurous culture that goes back to the **birthplace**[9] of adventure tourism in New Zealand— the **Kawarau**[10] Bridge. The bridge was the world's first **commercial**[11] bungee-jumping site.

Just like high wire bungee, bridge bungee jumping is a thrilling and slightly frightening sport. Therefore, jumping is sometimes a little difficult for people because they're so high up. As one person watching the jumpers says with a smile, "I think it's great— if someone else is doing it!"

---

[9]**birthplace:** place where someone or something was born or started
[10]**Kawarau:** [kɑwərau]
[11]**commercial:** used for making money

Back at the Nevis jump site, a young woman named **Marlene**[12] is finding out that it really isn't always easy to jump. She's very nervous and she's having difficulty getting out of the jump pod. It's easy to understand since the view looks very dangerous and frightening from the top! "Here we go Marlene," says the instructor, "lean forward; five, four, three, two, one!" Marlene finally jumps, crying out as she falls far below.

According to Henry Van Asch, "the people who have to really try hard to jump are the ones that get the most out of it." At least that's what some people think. It seems that for Marlene, it's a bit different. When the instructor asks, "How was that?" after her jump, Marlene replies, "I'm never bungee jumping again!" It doesn't look like Marlene will be bungee jumping again any time soon. But then, perhaps for some people, jumping once is enough!

---

[12] **Marlene:** [marlin]

What do you think?

1. Do you think bungee jumping is dangerous?

2. Would you like to bungee jump at least once? Why or why not?

3. Which of the sports in this story do you like most?

For most jumpers, at the end of the day, they're very happy that they've done it. "Okay, cheers!" says one jumper, as he **toasts**[13] his friend with a cool drink after their adventure. "Ah, we **deserve**[14] that," his friend replies. "That was a good one!" he adds, referring to the jump.

Here in Queenstown, the land that seems made for adventure, the only big question may be: What will they think of doing next? Whatever it is, you can be sure that someone in 'The Adventure Capital of the World' will be ready to give it a try!

---

[13]**toast:** lift your glass and drink with other people
[14]**deserve:** have earned something; be worthy of

After You Read

1. In paragraph 1 on page 4, the word 'cries' can be replaced by:
   A. tears
   B. whispers
   C. shouts
   D. songs

2. Henry thinks that people come to the Nevis High Wire site to bungee jump because:
   A. It's fun.
   B. The jump pod is little.
   C. It's dangerous.
   D. The drop is especially far.

3. Both men and women like to bungee _____.
   A. jumping
   B. jump
   C. jumper
   D. jumped

4. In paragraph 3 on page 6, 'them' refers to:
   A. people who love adventure
   B. New Zealanders
   C. Henry and his friends
   D. adventure sports

5. Which of the following is a good heading for page 8?
   A. New Zealand Adventure Invention
   B. Jetboat Uses New Style Propeller
   C. Spinning Machine
   D. Adventure Seekers Hate Boat

6. In paragraph 2 on page 8, the word 'thrill' describes a feeling of:
   A. fear
   B. danger
   C. excitement
   D. anger

7. How many different types of sports are there in Queenstown?
   A. two
   B. five
   C. eighty
   D. sixty

8. On page 12, the writer's purpose is to:
   A. introduce a new sport
   B. talk about tired hikers
   C. explain about a traditional adventure sport
   D. describe the environment around the city

9. On page 15, the person watching on the bridge probably thinks that bungee jumping is:
   A. easy
   B. extreme
   C. terrible
   D. boring

10. According to Henry Van Asch, which type of people get the most out of bungee jumping?
   A. people who are worried
   B. people who are excited
   C. people who are bored
   D. people who are happy

11. In paragraph 2 on page 19, who is 'they' referring to?
   A. the jumpers
   B. the tourists
   C. New Zealanders
   D. jetboat owners

12. Which of the following adventure sports is NOT mentioned in this story?
   A. helicopter rides
   B. bungee jumping
   C. hiking
   D. driving cars

Jetboats

A jetboat is a very special type of boat that can be used in very shallow water. It can be operated in as little as twelve inches of water. A jetboat can also make extremely tight turns. In addition, if the boat has openings on the sides, it can actually move through the water sideways, as well as forwards and backwards.

The History of the Jetboat

Two people were largely responsible for the development of this amazing machine. An Italian man named Secundo Campini had the idea first. In the 1930s and 1940s, he built and tested several jetboat models. However, it was Sir William Hamilton, a New Zealander, who was responsible for the popular jetboats today. The timeline below gives some of the important steps in the machine's development.

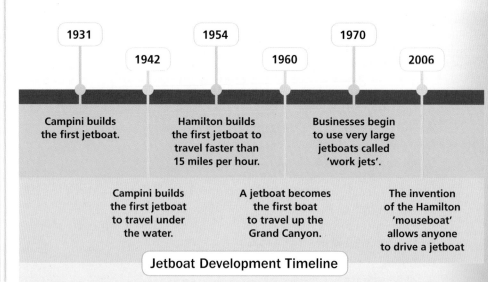

1931 — Campini builds the first jetboat.

1942 — Campini builds the first jetboat to travel under the water.

1954 — Hamilton builds the first jetboat to travel faster than 15 miles per hour.

1960 — A jetboat becomes the first boat to travel up the Grand Canyon.

1970 — Businesses begin to use very large jetboats called 'work jets'.

2006 — The invention of the Hamilton 'mouseboat' allows anyone to drive a jetboat

Jetboat Development Timeline

A jetboat can go almost anywhere.

The Mechanics of a Jetboat

A jetboat does not use a propeller to push itself through the water like other boats. Instead, it takes in water through a large opening under the boat. Then, it pushes the water out of a smaller hole at the back of the boat. This hole is below the level of the water. The action of the water leaving the small hole causes the boat to move forward. Most regular boats have propellers which extend below the bottom of the boat. Many also use a large board, called a 'rudder,' to turn right and left. A jetboat, on the other hand, has neither. Instead, jetboat drivers control the direction of the water as it leaves the smaller hole. This is how the driver guides the boat through the water. Because it doesn't have a propeller or rudder, a jetboat can operate in very shallow water and not hit anything below it.

CD 1, Track 08

Word Count: 345
Time: _____

Vocabulary List

adventure (2, 3, 4, 6, 8, 9, 11, 12, 15, 19)

birthplace (15)

bridge (2, 14, 15)

bring it on (6)

bungee jumping (2, 3, 4, 6, 8, 15, 16, 17)

capital (2, 11)

commercial (15)

crazy (4)

deserve (19)

frightening (3, 15, 16)

gap (4)

helicopter (2, 3, 12)

hike (2, 12, 13)

immediate lifestyle (6)

invention (8)

jetboat (3, 8, 9)

jump pod (4, 5, 6, 16)

pastime (2, 8)

propeller (3, 8)

proud (11)

shallow (3, 8)

spin 'em on a dime (8)

thrill (3, 8, 9, 15)

toast (19)